The Rules
of the Game

By Jennifer M. Sakurai
Illustrated by Jane Dierksen

PRICE STERN SLOAN
Los Angeles

ISBN: 0-8431-2430-X

10 9 8 7 6 5 4 3

The Rules of
the Game

This book is divided into three sections: major league
rules, Little League rules and definitions of baseball
terms. The Little League section covers only those rules
which differ from those in the major league. Otherwise, the rules in the major league section are the
same rules used by Little League teams.

The Playing Field

BASEBALL DIAMOND: The diamond is the same size in all ballparks. It is called a "baseball diamond" because the lines between the bases create a diamond shape. The first and third base lines extend beyond first and third base into the outfield, marking fair and foul territory. Vertical foul poles extend the lines into the bleachers. Any ball hit between the foul lines or poles is fair and in play.

INFIELD: There are many regulations about size and length of the diamond.

- The **bases** are 90 feet apart.
- The distance from the **pitcher's mound** to **home plate** is 60 feet 6 inches.
- The pitcher's mound must be exactly 10 inches high.
- The **batter's circle,** which also holds the catcher and umpire, has a 26-foot radius.
- Within the batter's circle are 2 **batter's boxes,** one for right-handed batters and one for left-

handed batters. The batter's boxes are on either side of home plate.

- The **on-deck circles** are 37 feet from the batter's circle. There is 1 on-deck circle for each team. Each circle is 5 feet in diameter. The next person at bat uses the on-deck circle as a place to warm up.

FOUL TERRITORY: The area outside the foul lines and foul poles is **foul territory.** The **backstop fence** is 60 feet behind home plate in foul territory. Fifteen feet behind both first and third base are **coaches' boxes,** which are 10 by 20 feet. The team at bat has a coach in each of these positions. Behind the coaches' boxes, cut into the stadium seats, are the teams' **dugouts.** Coaches, trainers and players who are not on the field must remain in their dugout during the game.

OUTFIELD: The distance from home plate to the outfield bleachers may vary from field to field, but the nearest boundary or fence in fair territory must be at least 250 feet away from home plate. Most stadiums have open areas between the outfield bleachers called **bullpens.** Relief pitchers warm up there before being called into the game.

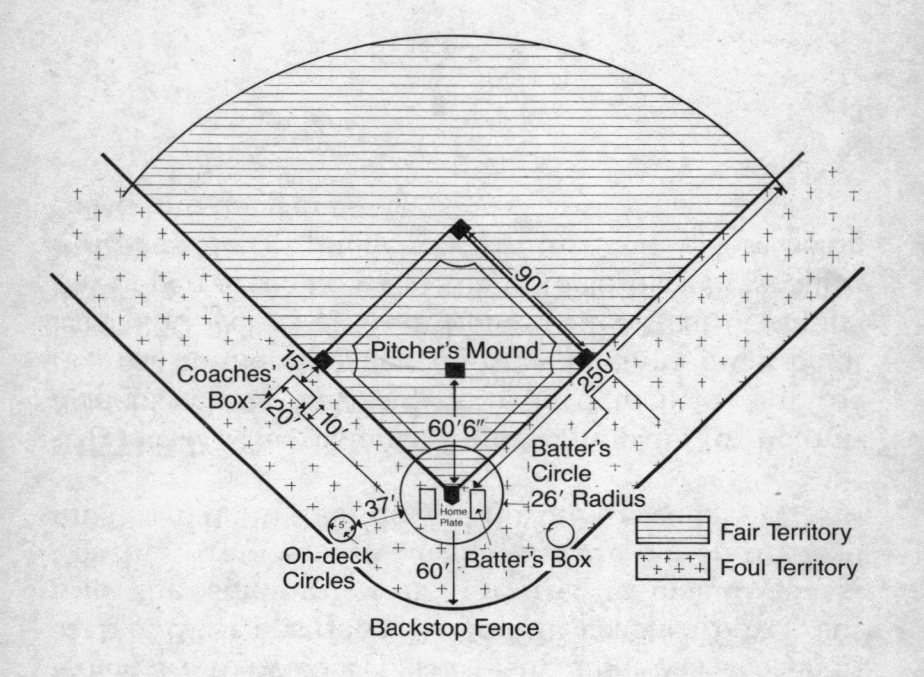

Major League Field

The Equipment

THE BALL: The baseball's core is made of rubber and cork. Yarn is wound around the rubber and cork center. Then 2 strips of white cowhide are sewn around the ball. Official baseballs must weigh 5 to 5¼ ounces and be 9 to 9¼ inches around.

THE BAT: A bat must be made of one or two pieces of wood. It must keep a natural wood color. The bat must be no longer than 42 inches and no wider than 2¾ inches. Players are allowed to cover the first 18 inches of the bat's handle so they can grip it better. Many players wrap tape on the handle.

GLOVES: Baseball gloves vary depending on the player's position.

- The **first baseman's** glove is a maximum of 8 inches wide and 12 inches long and does not have fingers.
- Other **fielders'** gloves have fingers and have a maximum width of 7¾ inches.

- The **pitcher's** glove must be one solid color, but it cannot be white or gray.

- The **catcher's** mitt can't be more than 38 inches around or be longer than 15½ inches.

The catcher and first baseman's gloves are largest because these players catch more balls than other fielders and recover more wild throws.

HELMETS: Batters are required to wear a helmet with an earflap. These helmets help protect players from injury. Earflaps are optional for players who were in the majors before the rule was adopted.

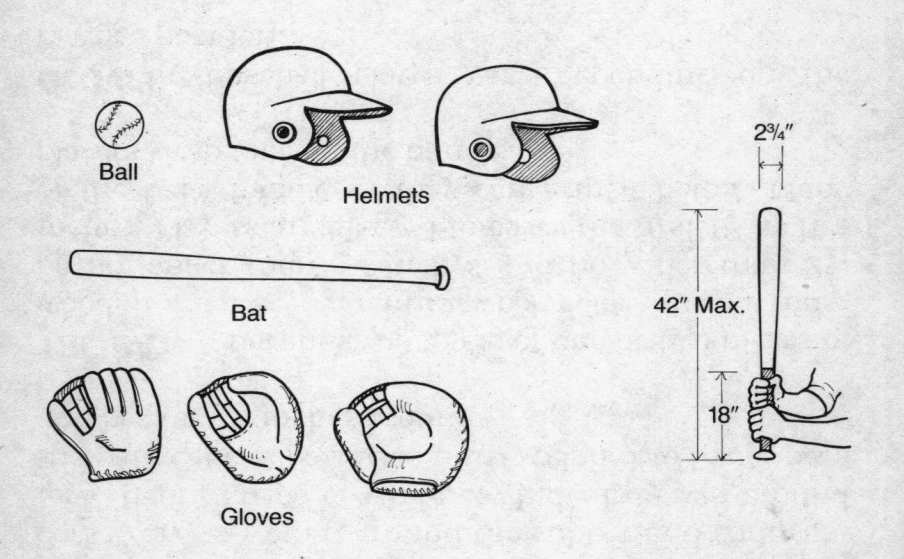

Ball

Helmets

Bat

2¾″

42″ Max.

18″

Gloves

Baseball Gear

CATCHER'S GEAR: Special gear helps protect the catcher from injury. All catchers wear a metal face mask, padded chest protector and plastic shin guards.

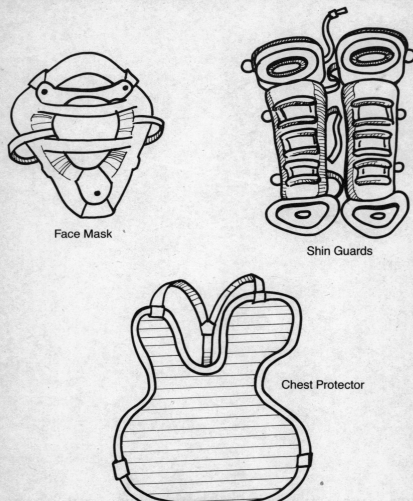

Face Mask

Shin Guards

Chest Protector

Catcher's Gear

TEAM UNIFORM: Each team has a uniform, including socks, knickers, a jersey and cap. All team members must wear the same uniform. Each team has a different dress code, such as how much of the players' socks can show, and even whether or not the men can have beards! Some of these club traditions are very old.

The People in Baseball

UMPIRES: Umpires are baseball's judges, calling strikes and balls, fair or foul, out or safe. They also have the authority to kick players out of a game for bad behavior or breaking the rules. Four umpires are in charge of each major-league game. They are positioned behind the plate, second base and down each foul line. During the World Series, there are 2 additional umpires down the foul line. Umpires can't be removed from a game except for medical reasons.

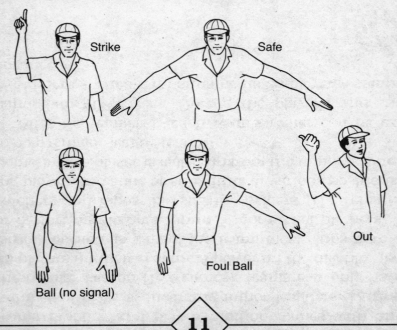

Strike

Safe

Out

Foul Ball

Ball (no signal)

PLAYERS: During spring training, major-league teams practice and play exhibition games with any number of players, including minor leaguers. During the regular season (162 games), teams can only have 25 players on their rosters. A player on the disabled list is not counted as part of the team. Most clubs have 4 or 5 starting pitchers, up to 5 more relief pitchers, 2 catchers and 7 possible starting fielders. The remaining players can start or substitute at various positions. Sometimes a player is called up from the minor leagues to help a major-league team.

After September 1, each team's roster can be expanded to 40 players. During the playoffs and the World Series, a team must name its 25-player roster in advance.

The Game

OBJECT OF THE GAME: In baseball, the team that has the most runs at the end of a game is the winner. A regular game has 9 innings. If there is a tie at the end of 9 innings, the game continues until there is a winner. Five innings must be completed for a **called game** to count in the standings.

A **called game** is a game stopped by the umpires for various reasons, such as rain. The game is played again later in the season if less than five innings were completed.

MAJOR LEAGUE

Scoreboard

INNINGS	1	2	3	4	5	6	7	8	9	TOTAL
VISITORS										
HOME										

Line-up Card

TEAM   DATE

NO.	PLAYER	POS.
1		
2		
3		
4		
5		
6		
7		
8		
9		
10		

ON THE BENCH

BEFORE THE GAME:

The Plate Umpire: Before the game begins, the plate (chief) umpire checks to make sure that the playing field is clearly marked and that the home team has supplied enough baseballs. There must be at least 12 balls available, and the umpire must carry at least 2 at all times. When the balls get dirty, they become dangerous because the players cannot see them easily. Damaged balls are harder to control. For these reasons, the balls are replaced often.

The Managers: Before play begins, the managers of both teams present the plate umpire with their batting orders. Managers also receive a copy of the opposing team's line-up. The umpire must be told when a **pinch hitter** or **pinch runner** enters a game.

A **pinch hitter** or **pinch runner** is a player who hits or runs in place of a teammate, especially when a hit or run is badly needed. The player who is replaced cannot return to the game.

The Pitchers: Before each inning, a pitcher is given 1 minute to throw a maximum of 8 warm-up pitches. Relief pitchers are also allowed 8 warm-up pitches when they first enter a game. If a pitcher is injured and no relievers are warmed up, the umpire may permit the reliever to throw more than 8 warm-up pitches from the mound.

The Catchers: When play begins, all fielders except the catcher must be in fair territory (the catcher's box is in foul ground). The catcher must remain in the box until the pitch is released. However, he or she may move out of the box to catch or throw a ball.

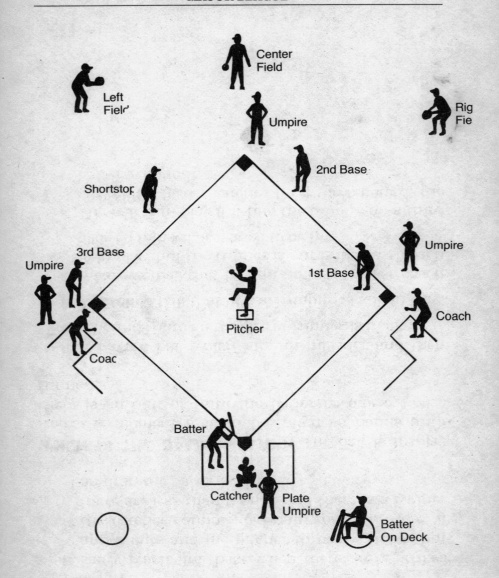

Field With Players

To get on base, a batter must:

- get a hit.
- draw a walk.
- be hit by a pitch.
- safely reach first base when there are 2 strikes and 2 outs and the pitcher throws a strike, but the catcher cannot hold onto the ball. (Note: If there are less than 2 outs, and there is a runner on first, the batter is out.)

WHEN IS THE BALL IN PLAY?: The ball is in play from the moment it is in the pitcher's hands until there is an out, or until the batter becomes a base runner.

- A **batted** ball which hits an infielder and then rebounds onto an umpire or runner is in play.
- A **pitched** ball that hits an umpire is still in play.
- A **thrown** ball that hits an umpire or base coach is in play, but the runner is out if the base coach allowed himself or herself to be hit.
- The ball is in play if it hits the umpire on a third strike. If a fielder catches it off the rebound, the batter is not out.

WHEN IS THE BALL DEAD?: The ball is dead when:

- it is hit into foul territory.
- the batter breaks a rule while hitting the ball (for example, stepping out of the batter's box).
- the umpire interferes with a catcher's attempt to throw out a base runner (if a runner is thrown out, the play counts; if the runner is safe, the batter is out).
- a pitch gets stuck in the plate umpire's equipment (runners advance one base).
- a **foul bunt** is hit off a third strike (the batter is out).
- it hits the umpire off a **foul tip** on a called third strike (the batter is not out).
- a foul tip gets stuck in the umpire's equipment (this is not a strike).

PITCHING: During an inning, a manager or coach is allowed one discussion with the pitcher. If a manager goes to the mound again, the pitcher must be removed from the game. If the manager waits to speak to the incoming reliever, that counts as a visit. A manager can't approach the mound more than once during the same at-bat or the umpire can bar him or her from the game. The pitcher then has to leave the game after the batter completes his or her turn.

Nothing can be put on the ball (such as petroleum jelly or hair oil), nor can the pitcher rub the ball across his glove or uniform. A pitcher may not spit in a glove or hand, or wipe his or her pitching hand over the mouth. If an umpire spots a player breaking one of these rules, he or she calls a ball. If the pitcher is caught again, he or she must leave the game.

When the umpire feels a pitcher has thrown the ball at the batter on purpose, he or she will warn the pitcher and both managers. If there is a second violation, the umpire can eject both the pitcher and his manager from the game.

BALK

When a **balk** is called, runners advance 1 base. The ball is dead unless the batter tries to reach first. If the batter reaches first and runners safely advance, the play counts. If the batter is out then the other runners advance the 1 base they are awarded on the balk.

A pitcher balks when he or she:

- drops the ball with runners on base.
- is not on the rubber when delivering a pitch.
- delays the game.
- releases a pitch while the catcher is out of the catcher's box.

- throws to an unoccupied base from the rubber.
- delivers the pitch in other than a set (standing) position or after a wind-up.

If a pitcher tries to pick off a base runner on first, he or she must step toward first base and complete the throw. The pitcher doesn't need to step toward second or third base, nor does he or she have to release the ball. However, if the pitcher fakes to one base but throws to another, he or she must step toward the base being thrown to or be called for a balk.

When the base runner takes a lead off the base, the pitcher may try a pick-off in the middle of a pitch. He or she must step toward the base while throwing or a balk will be charged. If the pitcher drops the ball and there are no base runners, the ball is dead. However, if the baseball crosses the foul line, the pitch is called a ball. If there are players on base when the ball is dropped, a balk is called.

BATTING: Players bat in the batting order given to the umpire before the game. However, if the last out of an inning involved a runner and not the batter, that batter returns in the next inning and starts over.

A batter can't leave the batter's box unless the umpire has granted a time out. Otherwise, any pitch except a balk will count. If the batter is out of the box when he hits a pitch, he or she is called out if the opposing team appeals. An umpire may not call time in the middle of a pitch.

- A batter is out after three strikes, if tagged or thrown out while base running, or if a fly ball is caught.

- If a batter is hit by his or her own fair ball before an infielder touches it, the batter is out unless he or she is still in the batter's box.

- If the batted ball hits a runner under the **infield fly rule,** the runner is safe only if he or she is standing on the base.

Infield Fly Rule: A play called by the umpire when he or she believes that a fly ball can be caught easily. This rule is used when there are less than 2 outs and the bases are loaded, or there are runners on first and second. The rule was created for the runner's protection against a fielder's "error." This play prevents an infielder from dropping the ball on purpose, hoping to move runners off base to be tagged or thrown out. With this rule, the batter is automatically out. Runners may advance *if they wish*, but it is difficult to advance while the ball is in the infield in someone's possession.

- A batter is sent to first base if he or she is hit by a pitch as long as the batter tried to avoid the ball. This rule does not count if the pitch was in the **strike zone,** regardless of the batter's attempt to avoid being hit.

- If the batter doesn't try to avoid contact and is hit outside the strike zone, a ball will be counted.

The **strike zone** is the area over home plate be-tween the batter's armpits and knees when the batter is positioned to swing. Any pitch deliv-ered through this area is a strike.

BASE RUNNING: Runners should never interfere with a fielder pursuing the ball. A runner can get called out for running outside of the base lines, but this rule does not count when the runner has to go around a fielder who is trying to make a play. A batter can also be called out if an umpire feels that a runner interfered with a fielder's play on purpose.

When a fielder throws an object at a fair **batted** ball, the umpire awards the batter and runners 3 bases and the ball remains in play.

If a fielder throws an object at a **thrown** ball or accidentally throws a ball out of the field of play, the umpire awards the batter and runners 2 bases.

If a wild pitch goes into the dugout or stands, or gets stuck in the screen or rolls under it, runners ad-vance 1 base. If a fielder falls into the stands or dugout after catching a ball, runners advance 1 base. If the fielder in the stands or dugout doesn't fall, the ball is in play. Runners may try to advance, but can be tagged or thrown out.

A runner can be thrown out whenever he or she steps off the base. Any runs that are scored before a runner gets thrown out count. In order for a runner to advance on a fly ball, runners must wait until the ball is caught before they leave their bases. If a runner has a lead off the base *before* the ball is caught, he or she must return and tag the base *after* the ball is caught before advancing.

Runners can steal second or third base whenever the ball is in play and in the pitcher's possession. However, runners trying to steal may be thrown or tagged out.

A runner on third base can try to **steal home** base. If the runner is hit by a ball pitched in the strike zone at a 2 out, 2 strike count, the batter is out, the run doesn't score and the inning ends. If there are less than 2 outs, the batter is out, but the run counts.

INTERFERENCE: When a broken bat hits a ball, runner or fielder in fair ground, there is no interference. If a whole bat flies out of a batter's hands and interferes with a play, the batter is out. *If there are less than 2 outs and a batter interferes with a fielder trying to make a play at home, the runner is out.* If there are 2 outs, the batter is out. If a batter interferes with a catcher, the ball is dead and the batter is out unless the catcher throws out a runner.

A runner who collides with a fielder is out if the collision prevents the fielder from getting the ball. A runner legally on base is safe if the play was unavoidable.

When a runner interferes with the ball in an attempt to break up a double play, that runner *plus* the runner closest to scoring are out and no one else may advance. If a runner is out and then interferes with a play involving another runner, the second runner is out.

OBSTRUCTION: If a fielder doesn't have the ball when he or she blocks a runner, the umpire charges the fielder with obstruction and stops play. All runners advance to the bases they would have reached on the play.

A catcher shouldn't block home plate from a runner unless he or she has the ball. However, sometimes the catcher stands in front of the plate to catch the ball. The umpire rarely calls obstruction on this play unless the catcher is trying to make the play harder for the runner.

If any fielder blocks the plate or touches the batter or bat when a runner is attempting to steal home, the run scores and the batter is awarded first base. The pitcher is charged with a balk if the catcher caused the play.

The Playing Field

INFIELD:

- In Little League, the **bases** are 60 feet apart.
- The distance from the **pitcher's mound** to **home plate** is 46 feet.
- The pitcher's mound is 6 inches high.
- The **batter's circle** has an 18-foot radius.
- The 2 **batter's boxes** are 6 by 3 feet long each.

FOUL TERRITORY: Little League rules suggest that there should be at least 25 feet between home plate and the backstop fence. There should also be 25 feet between the 2 base lines and the dugouts, spectator seats or any fencing. A fence 6 feet high guards each of the dugouts to protect players from injury. The coaching boxes are 4 by 8 feet long. They are at least 6 feet into foul territory behind both first and third base.

OUTFIELD: There should be at least 200 feet between home plate and any fence or other boundary in fair territory. The rules suggest that ball parks have an outfield fence that is 4 feet high.

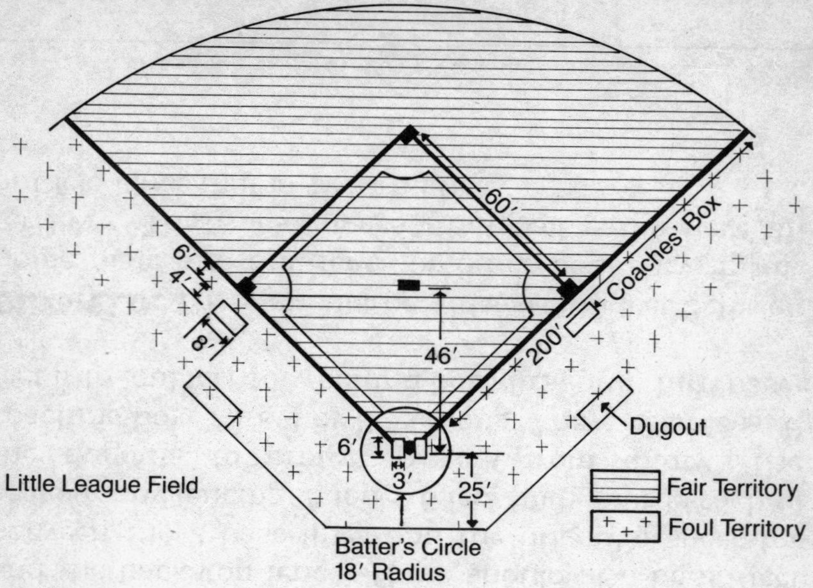

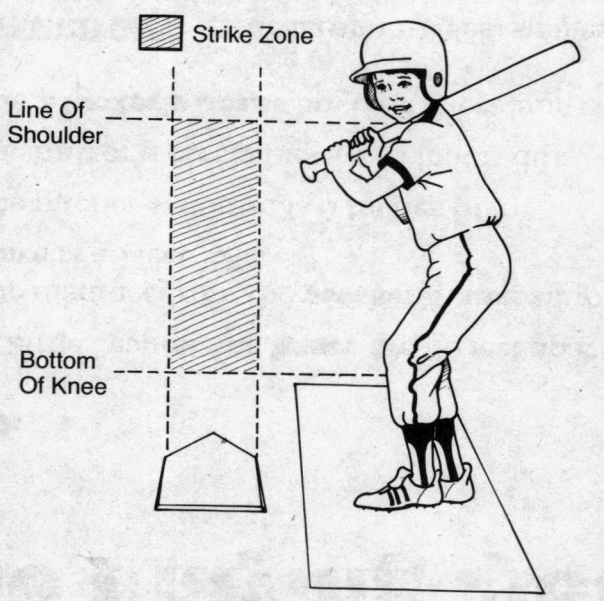

60'

200'

46'

6'
4'

8'

6'
3'

25'

Coaches' Box

Dugout

Little League Field

Fair Territory

Foul Territory

Batter's Circle
18' Radius

Strike Zone

Line Of
Shoulder

Bottom
Of Knee

The Equipment

THE BAT: The bat must be no longer than 33 inches and no wider than 2¼ inches. Players are allowed to cover the first 16 inches of the handle. Bats may be colored, but cannot be laminated.

GLOVES:

- The **catcher's** mitt may be any size, shape or weight, as long as it protects the hand.
- The rules covering the **fielders'** and **pitcher's** gloves are the same as in the majors.

HELMETS: The player on deck, the batter, and all base runners and player-coaches on the field must wear helmets. The helmet is optional for adult coaches.

TEAM UNIFORM: All team members must wear the same uniform. Players may not wear watches, pins, jewelry or other metal objects during the game. Coaches and managers may not wear the team uniform. They should wear pants and a shirt. They may, however, wear the team's cap.

The People in Baseball

UMPIRES: There are 1 or more umpires at every game. If there is only 1 umpire, he or she usually stands behind the catcher. When there are base runners, the umpire may choose to move behind the pitcher for a better overall view of the field. When there are 2 or more umpires, the chief umpire stays behind the plate. The other umpire(s) may stand anywhere on the field.

PLAYERS: Each team may have 12 to 15 players on its roster. Any member of the team may pitch. A maximum of 8 players may have a Little League age of 12. If a player is ill, injured or leaves the team during the season, the manager is allowed to find a replacement. Members may not play on any other baseball team during the Little League season except for official school teams.

To be chosen for a team, a player must attend at least half of the spring training sessions. Exceptions to this rule may be made in cases of illness or injury.

The Game

Anyone older than 9 and younger than 13 on August 1 may play on a Little League team during that calendar year. A player's age on August 1 is called his or her "Little League age." Children 8 to 12 years of age can play on a minor-league team if they are not chosen for a regular team.

Players between the ages of 6 and 8 play on Tee-Ball teams. The game is similar to baseball except that balls are hit off a batting tee rather than being thrown to the batter.

Senior League teams are made up of 13- to 15-year-old players. Junior League includes only 13 year olds because it is a minor-league division of Senior League. Big League team members are 16 to 18 years old.

OBJECT OF THE GAME: The object of the game is to score more runs than the opponent. Little League games are 6 innings long. At least 4 innings must be completed in a called game for the score to be official.

PLAYER PARTICIPATION: Every player must have at least one at bat and play at least 6 defensive outs every game. Any player who does not meet this rule is allowed to start the next game. The manager can be warned or punished for not allowing each member to play the minimum amount required. Team members are also allowed to act as base coaches.

Players who pitch less than 4 innings during 1 game must rest at least 1 day before pitching again. Throwing 1 pitch in an inning is counted as a full inning of pitching. If a player pitches more than 4 innings in 1 game, then 3 rest days must be taken.

In Little League, a pitcher is never allowed to pitch more than 6 innings a week (Sunday through Saturday). Only 2 pitchers of league age 12 can pitch for the same team during a week. No more than 5 pitchers may be used by one team during a game. If the fifth pitcher is injured, a sixth pitcher can be substituted.

SUBSTITUTIONS: In Little League, starting players can rejoin a game, but only if their substitute has had at least 1 at bat and has played 6 or more defensive outs. A replaced pitcher can't rejoin the game as a pitcher.

If a starter joins the game for a second time, but is later replaced by another substitute, the starter may not enter the game a third time. Only if a player is ill or injured and all the substitutes have been used can a starter join a third time. If a player has been kicked out of the game, a manager is not allowed to fill the position with anyone who has already played.

SEASON: The Little League season does not generally start before May. The season ends before the beginning of the school year. Each team should play at least 2 regular games a week and at least 12 games a season. Double-headers are not allowed. The rules suggest that the season be divided into 2 halves. The winners of each half then play against each other in a series at the end of the season to decide the league champion.

WHEN IS THE BALL IN PLAY? The rules are basically the same as those in the majors.

- A **batted** ball which hits an infielder and then rebounds onto an umpire or runner is in play.

- A **pitched** ball that hits an umpire is still in play.

- A **thrown** ball that hits an umpire or base coach is in play, but the runner is out if the base coach allowed himself to be hit.

- The ball is in play if it hits the umpire on a third strike. If a fielder catches it off the rebound, the batter is not out.

However, if a batter swings at strike 3 and is hit by the ball (dead ball), he or she is out.

PITCHING: A coach or manager can make 2 trips to the pitching mound per inning to talk to the pitcher. If the pitcher is approached a third time, he or she must leave the game. The 3 trips to the mound cannot be made during the same at bat. Only the catcher may join these talks.

BALK

The rules for balking are the same in Little League as they are in the majors. However, in Little League, a balk is also called anytime the pitcher drops the ball while standing on the plate. The pitcher must always step towards any base he or she is throwing to.

BATTING: All team members must have at least 1 at bat per game. A player is called out for swinging at strike 3 even if he or she is hit by the ball.

Definitions of Baseball Terms

Appeal: A complaint to the umpire that the opposing team has broken a rule, or a complaint about an umpire's call (decision).

Bail out: To step back while swinging at a pitch.

Balk: There are many different ways a pitcher can balk. For example, when the pitcher starts a delivery to the plate or to first base, then stops, the umpire calls a balk. When a balk is called, runners advance a base.

Ball: A pitch outside the strike zone.

Base coach: A coach who stands by first or third base. The base coaches instruct the batter and base runners with a series of hand signals.

Base hit: A play in which the batter hits the ball in fair territory and reaches first base before being thrown out. Also called a **single.**

Battery: A term referring to the pitcher and catcher.

Batting average: A player's hitting percentage compared to his or her total number of at bats.

Bunt: A batter bunts by sliding his or her top hand near the middle of the bat and holding the bat parallel to the ground. A good bunter keeps the ball low to the ground and hard to field.

Bunt

Called game: A game suspended or ended by the umpire.

Checked swing: A partial swing. If the swing has gone more than halfway around, the umpire can rule it a full swing, or strike.

Count: The number of called balls and strikes on a batter.

Dead ball: A ball out of play. For example, a ball hit into the seats in foul territory, out of the reach of the defensive team.

Defensive team: The teams playing on the field: the battery, infielders and outfielders.

Designated hitter (DH): A player who bats in the pitcher's spot in the line-up. The DH does not have a fielding position. The designated hitter rule is only used in the American League.

Double: A hit that enables a batter to reach second base.

Double-header: Two games played back to back by the same teams.

Double play: Any defensive play that ends in 2 base runners being called out.

Earned run: A run scored on a hit, walk or steal, without a defensive error on the play.

Earned run average: The average number of runs per game a pitcher has allowed during the season.

Error: A defensive mistake that allows a batter to stay at the plate or reach first base, or that advances a base runner.

Fielder's choice: Term used when a fielder can choose among base runners to throw or tag out.

Force play (or force-out): This play occurs when a runner is forced to advance because there is another runner behind him or her, even when he or she will be thrown or tagged out.

Forfeited game: A forfeited game is awarded to a team because of a penalty to its opponents. A team can be awarded a game even if it was losing or had lost. Forfeited games do not have to be completed. The score of a forfeited game is 9-0.

Foul ball: A ball hit into foul territory.

Foul tip: A ball that lands directly in the catcher's mitt after touching the bat. This counts as a strike unless the catcher drops a foul tip on the third strike.

Grand slam: A grand slam is a home run hit when there is a runner on every base. This hit scores 4 runs.

Green light: A signal from the coach to hit the next good pitch, or a signal to a base runner that gives the runner the authority to decide when to attempt a steal.

Ground rule double: A hit which is ruled a double because of interference. The umpire calls for a ground rule double if he or she thinks that a hit would have been a double or more if there had not been any inter-ference. A ground rule double is also called after a ball bounces into the stands from fair territory, and when a fan touches a ball in play.

Home run: A ball hit out of the playing field in fair territory. A home run scores the batter and any base runners.

Infield fly rule: A play called by the umpire when he or she believes that a fly ball can be caught easily. This rule is used when there are less than 2 outs and the bases are loaded, or there are runners on first and second. The rule was created for the runner's protec-tion against a fielder's "error." This play prevents an infielder from dropping the ball on purpose, hoping to move runners off base to be tagged or thrown out. With this rule, the batter is automatically out. Runners may advance *if they wish* but it is difficult to advance while the ball is in the infield in someone's possession.

Inning: A period of play. There are 9 innings in a regulation game. Each team bats in an inning until they record 3 outs. The visiting team always bats in the top half (beginning) of an inning. If the home team has a higher total after their opponents bat in the top half of the ninth inning, the bottom half of the inning is not played and the score is final. A tie at the end of regulation play forces extra innings. The game con-tinues until an inning is complete and the visitors have a higher score, or until the home team breaks the tie (then they do not complete the 3 outs).

Iron mike: A mechanical pitching machine used in practice.

Jam: A technique used by pitchers when they throw the ball close to the batters to jam their swings. The ball hits the bat's handle and can't travel far.

Leg out a hit: To beat an infield roller to first.

Line drive: A ball hit directly to a fielder.

Line-up: A team's batting order.

Offensive team: The team up at bat.

Official scorer: The person who compiles the official record of the game. He or she decides whether to credit plays with a hit or an error.

On deck: A term used to refer to the next batter up in the inning. This person stands in the on-deck circle and warms up. If the inning ends before his or her turn, he or she will start the next inning.

Out in order: To retire the 3 starting batters in an inning.

Passed ball: A pitched ball which gets away from the catcher, allowing a runner to advance.

Pinch hitter: A hitter who substitutes in the line-up. The original batter can't return to the game, so the pinch hitter or a third person takes over the defensive position as well.

Pinch runner: A player entering the game to run for someone already on base. See **pinch hitter** for rules regarding defensive replacement.

Pitchout: When a pitch is thrown wide of the strike zone on purpose. Sometimes a catcher calls for a pitchout if he or she thinks that a runner is trying to steal.

Relief pitcher: The pitcher replacing the starter. The relief pitcher can win, lose, save, or not be involved in the game's final score.

Reverse force double play: A double play in which the first play is a force-out and the second is a tag-out.

Rookie: A player in his first complete season in the major leagues. Also, players who spend only part of the year in the majors (for example, to replace an injured or ill player).

Run: A score obtained when a base runner safely crosses home plate.

Run down: A play used by fielders to tag out a runner caught between bases.

Runs batted in (RBI or "ribby"): A statistic which shows how often a player has made it possible for his or her teammates to score while at bat. A player who has 30 RBI's has caused 30 runs to score. A batter is not credited with an RBI if he or she hit into a double play or if the run scored because of an error.

Sacrifice: A bunt designed to advance a runner although the batter will be thrown out.

Sacrifice fly: A fly ball out that scores a runner from third base.

Save: A relief pitcher gets a save if he or she can keep the team's lead while the opponent's tying or winning runs are on base, or if he or she pitches 3 or more innings without allowing the opponents to tie the game.

Scoring position: A runner on second or third base.

Seventh inning stretch: A baseball tradition; fans stand after the top half of the seventh inning to sing "Take Me Out to the Ball Game."

Shoestring catch: Catching a line drive or fly ball just before it hits the ground.

Shutout: A game in which one team doesn't score any runs.

Single: See **base hit.**

Slide: A technique used to avoid being tagged out or to interfere with a throw. Base runners slide by throwing themselves at a base instead of running to tag it. Most players slide feet first.

Squeeze play: A play that can be used to get a runner home from third base. The batter must bunt down the first base line. The ball should drop directly between home plate and the fielders so the runner has enough time to score. It is best to use this play when there are less than 2 outs. If the batter hits the ball to a fielder by mistake, the runner at third can remain on base. The batter will be tagged or thrown out and the next batter can try to advance the runner.

Spring training: Before the regular season starts, teams gather in spring training camps to train and play exhibition games.

Steal: Successfully advancing a base between pitches without a base hit by a teammate.

Strike: A strike is called if a batter swings at a pitch and misses, or if the pitch simply passes through the strike zone. If the batter is called out on strikes without swinging at the last pitch, he or she is "caught looking." The first 2 foul balls that are not caught count as first and second strikes. A foul ball that is not caught can never be counted as a third strike.

Strike out the side: Striking out the last batter in the inning.

Strike zone: The area over home plate between the batter's armpits and knees when the batter is positioned to swing. Any pitch that is delivered through this area is called a strike. The shorter the batter, the smaller the strike zone.

Suspended game: A game stopped by the head umpire and finished on another day. Reasons may include bad weather, or time considerations in an extra inning game.

Tag: An action runners must perform before they can advance on a fly ball. Runners must tag the base they occupy *after* the ball is caught before they can try to advance. Runners can leave their base before a ball is hit, but must return and tag the base if the ball is caught.

Time Out: Any umpire can call a time out because of weather, injury, foreign objects on the playing field, etc. Managers and players can ask an umpire to call a time out.

Trapped ball: When a fielder doesn't catch the ball, but traps it between the glove and the ground. The batter is not out and the ball is still in play. Runners may try to advance if they wish.

Triple: A hit enabling the batter to safely reach third base.

Triple play: A defensive play that records 3 outs.

Walk: An award given to the batter after the pitcher delivers 4 balls. If a hitter receives 4 balls during an at bat, he or she automatically advances to first base. Any forced base runners advance. Also called **base on balls.**

Wild pitch: A pitch so far from the strike zone that the catcher cannot catch or block it.